About Insects

About Insects

A Guide for Children

Cathryn Sill

Illustrated by John Sill

PEACHTREE

ATLANTA

For the One who created insects.

—*Genesis* 1:25

Ω

Published by
PEACHTREE PUBLISHERS, LTD.
1700 Chattahoochee Avenue
Atlanta, Georgia 30318-2112
www.peachtree-online.com

Text © 2000 Cathryn P. Sill
Jacket and interior illustrations © 2000 John C. Sill

First trade paperback edition published 2003

Jacket illustration by John Sill

Manufactured in Singapore

10 9 8 7 6 5 4 3 2 (hardcover edition)
10 9 8 7 6 5 4 3 2 1 (trade paperback edition)

Library of Congress Cataloging-in-Publication Data

Sill, Cathryn P., 1953–
    About insects: a guide for children / Cathryn Sill; illustrated by John Sill.
        p. cm.
    Summary: Describes the anatomy, behavior, and habitat of various
    insects, including the beetle, moth, and cockroach.

    ISBN 1-56145-207-6 (hardcover)
    ISBN 1-56145-232-7 (trade paperback)

    1. Insects—Juvenile literature. [1. Insects.] I. Sill, John, ill. II. Title.

QL467.2 .S538 2000
595.7—dc21
                            99-045785

About Insects

Insects have six legs...

PLATE 1
Dogbane Leaf Beetle

and three body parts.

PLATE 2
Cow Killer

They have a waterproof skeleton on the outside of their bodies.

PLATE 3
Elephant Stag Beetle

Young insects hatch from eggs.

PLATE 4
Praying Mantis

They go through several changes before becoming adults.

PLATE 5
Monarch Butterfly

Antennae help insects smell and feel.

Some insects suck animals or plants
to get nourishment.

Others bite and chew their food.

PLATE 8
Southeastern Lubber Grasshopper

Many insects fly.

PLATE 9
White Tail

Some crawl because they have no wings.

Others jump...

or swim.

Insects live almost everywhere.

PLATE 13
Silverfish

Some are active during the day.

PLATE 14
Honey Bee

Others are active only at night.

PLATE 15
Luna Moth

Some insects may be pests.

PLATE 16
German Cockroach

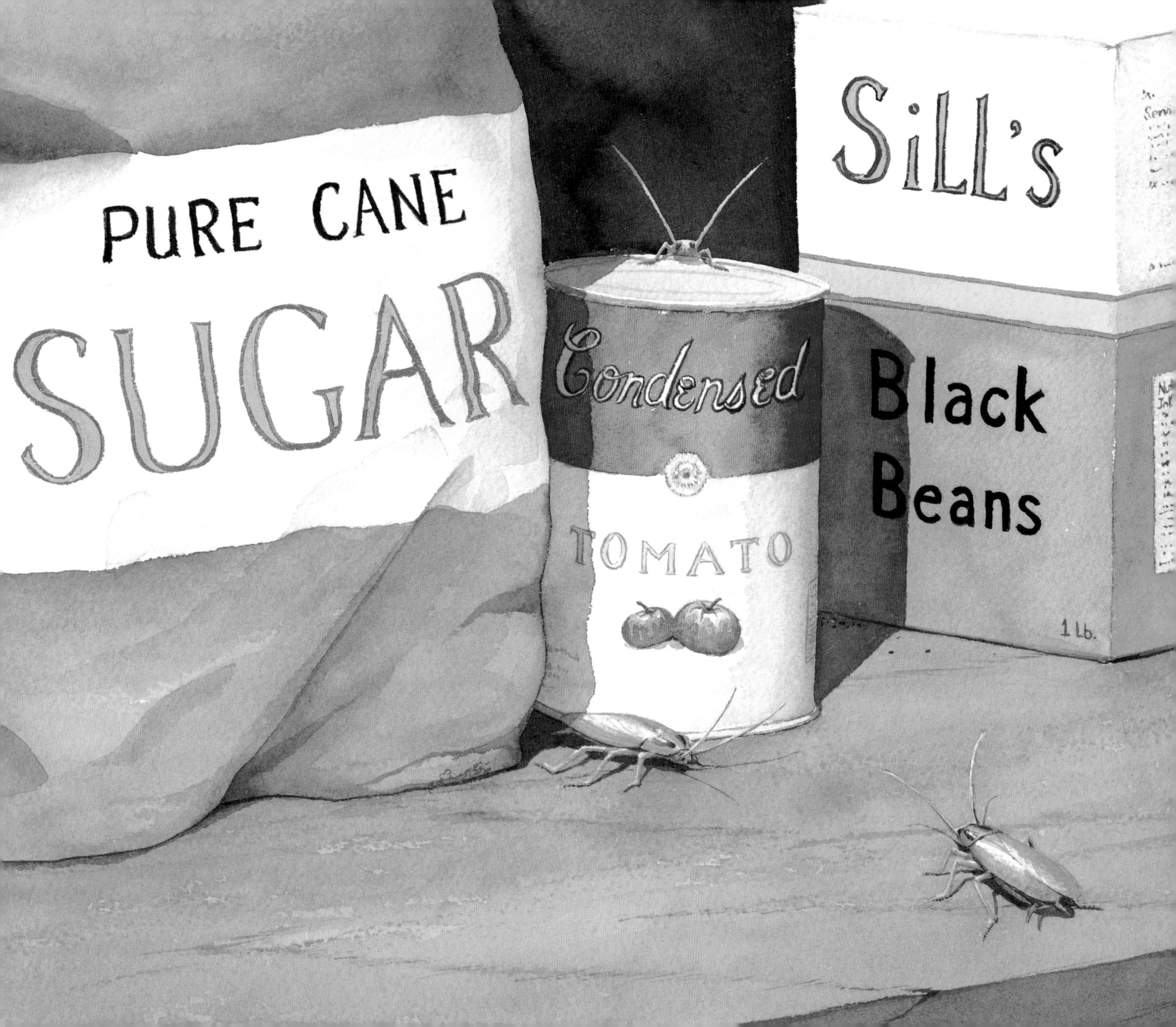
PURE CANE
SUGAR
Condensed
TOMATO
SiLL's
Black
Beans
1 Lb.

But many are very helpful.

Insects are an important part of our world.

Afterword

PLATE 1

Insects are the most numerous of all animals. Over 1,000,000 species have been identified, four times more than all other animals combined. There are nearly 100,000 species of insects in North America. Insects are arthropods, which are animals with distinctly divided body parts, jointed legs, and a hard outer coating called an exoskeleton. Insects have three pairs of legs and three body parts. Dogbane Leaf Beetles discharge a foul-smelling secretion if caught.

PLATE 2

An insect's body is made up of three major parts—the head, the thorax, and the abdomen. The antennae, eyes, and mouthparts are located on the head. The legs and wings are attached to the thorax. The abdomen contains the digestive and reproductive systems. Cow Killers are antlike wasps that get their name from their painful sting.

PLATE 3

Insects have hard coverings called exoskeletons. "Exo" means outside. The insect's muscles are attached to the inner surface of the exoskeleton. Stag beetles get their name from their huge mandibles, or jaws, which resemble the antlers of a stag.

PLATE 4

Insects grow by a process called metamorphosis. Some insects, such as the Praying Mantis, develop by simple or incomplete metamorphosis. They go through three stages of growth—egg, nymph, and adult. An adult female Praying Mantis lays hundreds of eggs in large masses covered with a protective foam that repels birds. Each egg hatches into a nymph, which resembles a small version of the adult. The nymph grows larger through a series of size changes until it reaches adulthood.

PLATE 5

Butterflies and many other insects develop by complete metamorphosis. They go through four distinct stages of development—egg, larva, pupa, and adult. An adult lays an egg, which produces a wormlike larva. The larva feeds and grows, then transforms into a pupa, which stays dormant for some period of time. When development of the pupa is complete, an adult insect emerges. Monarch Butterflies are the only butterflies that annually migrate both north and south.

PLATE 6

Insects smell, feel, and sometimes hear through sensory organs called antennae. Antennae are usually located on the front of the head. The structure of antennae varies greatly among insects. Virginia Ctenuchid Moths have feathery antennae.

PLATE 7
Most flies have mouthparts that lap up liquids. Black Horse Fly females suck blood from large mammals after slicing the skin with bladelike mouthparts. Males drink nectar from flowers.

PLATE 8
Insects that bite and chew their food do so by moving their mandibles from side to side. Southeastern Lubber Grasshoppers live on roadsides, in field edges, and in gardens where they feed on many kinds of leafy, green plants.

PLATE 9
Most adult insects have two pairs of wings attached to the thorax. Some insects have only one pair of wings, and some have no wings and are unable to fly. Dragonflies have four wings that move independently, enabling them to fly backward as well as forward. White Tails catch and eat small insects while in flight.

PLATE 10

Some insects mimic parts of the plants on which they live. The Giant Walkingstick looks so much like a twig that it is easily overlooked by predators. Walkingsticks are inactive during the day, but at night they move about, feeding on foliage.

PLATE 11

Powerful muscles in their hind legs enable some insects to be active jumpers. Gladiator Katydids live in grasslands or along roadsides, where they feed on grass.

PLATE 12

Beetles that live in lakes, ponds, rivers, and streams have paddle-shaped hind legs specially adapted to help them swim. Small Whirligig Beetles often swim in circles on the surface of the ponds and streams where they live. They are also able to dive below the surface.

PLATE 13
Insects live in almost every environment except the ocean. They have not been able to adapt to life in saltwater. Silverfish are found all over the world in warm, dark places, where they eat clothing, dry foods, and starch from bookbindings.

PLATE 14
Honey Bees are "social insects." Many of them live together in large nests and work together to preserve the colony. A queen lays all the eggs for the colony. The workers are females, and they maintain the hive and produce honey. The few male drones in each colony mate with the queen and then die.

PLATE 15
Most moths are nocturnal, or active at night. Adult Luna Moths live for only a short time and do not feed. Adult Luna Moth caterpillars eat the foliage of several kinds of trees, including walnut, sweet gum, and birch. Luna Moths are considered an endangered species because many have been killed by pollutants and insecticides.

PLATE 16

Insects can damage valuable crops and trees. Bites or stings from some insects can be irritating to mammals. Certain insects are responsible for spreading disease. Others infest food supplies or destroy clothing and wooden structures. Cockroaches have an unpleasant odor and scavenge in homes, restaurants, and food factories.

PLATE 17

Many insects help humans by eating other insects that destroy crops. Ladybug larvae and adults eat aphids and other small insects. Farmers and gardeners often purchase ladybugs and release them near crops that are harmed by aphids.

PLATE 18

Insects are a crucial food source for many animals that are valuable to us. They pollinate many of the plants that provide food for us. Useful products such as honey, beeswax, and silk are produced by insects. Some people are fascinated by insects and enjoy observing their unique habits.

Cathryn Sill is an elementary school teacher in Franklin, North Carolina, and the author of ABOUT BIRDS, ABOUT MAMMALS, ABOUT REPTILES, ABOUT FISH, ABOUT AMPHIBIANS, and ABOUT ARACHNIDS. With her husband John and her brother-in-law Ben Sill, she coauthored the popular bird-guide parodies A FIELD GUIDE TO LITTLE-KNOWN AND SELDOM-SEEN BIRDS OF NORTH AMERICA, ANOTHER FIELD GUIDE TO LITTLE-KNOWN AND SELDOM-SEEN BIRDS OF NORTH AMERICA, and BEYOND BIRDWATCHING, all from Peachtree Publishers.

John Sill is a prize-winning and widely published wildlife artist who illustrated ABOUT BIRDS, ABOUT MAMMALS, ABOUT REPTILES, ABOUT AMPHIBIANS, ABOUT FISH, and ABOUT ARACHNIDS, and illustrated and coauthored the FIELD GUIDES and BEYOND BIRDWATCHING. A native of North Carolina, he holds a B.S. in Wildlife Biology from North Carolina State University.